A LITTLE BIT OF CRICKET WIT

Summersdale Publishers Ltd
46 West Street
Chichester
West Sussex
PO19 1RP
UK

www.summersdale.com

Printed and bound in Malta

ISBN: 978-1-78685-251-9

Substantial discounts on bulk quantities of Summersdale books are available to corporations, professional associations and other organisations. For details contact general enquiries: telephone: +44 (0) 1243 771107 or email: enquiries@summersdale.com.

CONTENTS

EDITOR'S NOTE

HRH The Duke of Edinburgh once scoffed at the 'widely held and quite erroneous belief that cricket is just another game'. This eclectic compendium, for its part, aptly disproves such misconceptions, showing how the gentleman's game has inspired both profound insights and some outrageously funny off-the-cuff humour.

The delightful mix of run-out rebuttals, wicket wisecracks and 'howzat' humiliations in this side-splitting book will ensure you will never be stumped for a witty retort again.

A
HEAVENLY
GAME

Cricket – it's more than a game.
It's an institution.
THOMAS HUGHES

Watching cricket has given me
more happiness than any other
activity in which I have engaged.
A. A. MILNE

I AM CONFIDENT THEY PLAY CRICKET IN HEAVEN. WOULDN'T BE HEAVEN OTHERWISE, WOULD IT?

Patrick Moore

In my opinion cricket is too great a game to think about statistically.

E. H. HENDREN

Cricket is indescribable. How do you describe an orgasm?

GREG MATTHEWS

YESTERDAY AT THE OVAL HAD TO BE THE MOST THRILLING MOMENT OF MY LIFE... PERHAPS AFTER THE BIRTH OF MY CHILDREN.

Gladstone Small

CAPITAL GAIN – SMART SPORT – FINE EXERCISE – VERY.

Charles Dickens on cricket

The love of cricket nowadays seems to be confined to those who watch it or read about it.

ARTHUR MAILEY

If I knew I was going to die today, I'd still want to hear the cricket scores.

J. H. HARDY

GOING
BATTY

David Gower makes batting look
as easy as drinking tea.

LEONARD HUTTON

It's hard work making
batting look effortless.

DAVID GOWER

I COULDN'T BAT FOR THE LENGTH OF TIME REQUIRED TO SCORE 500. I'D GET BORED AND FALL OVER.

Denis Compton

It's like Manchester United getting a penalty and Bryan Robson taking it with his head.

DAVID LLOYD ON THE REVERSE SWEEP

My immediate objective was to hit the ball to each of the four corners of the field. After that, I tried not to be repetitive!

LEARIE CONSTANTINE

TEST CRICKET IS BLOODY HARD WORK, ESPECIALLY WHEN YOU'VE GOT SACHIN BATTING WITH WHAT LOOKS LIKE A THREE-METRE-WIDE BAT.

Michael Hussey

THEY CAME TO SEE ME BAT, NOT TO SEE YOU BOWL.

W. G. Grace on refusing to leave the crease having been bowled out by the first ball

His bowling is like shooting down F-16s with sling shots. Even if they hit, no damage would be done.

COLIN CROFT ON ANGUS FRASER IN THE GUYANA TEST

Spin bowling is like a software. If you don't try to upgrade it, you will fall by the wayside.

RAVICHANDRAN ASHWIN

I DON'T WANT TO DO THE BATSMAN ANY PERMANENT INJURY, JUST TO CAUSE HIM CONCERN – TO HURT HIM A BIT.

Dennis Lillee

There's nothing wrong with being aggressive – the bloke down the other end has a bat, some pads and a helmet.

SIMON JONES

To be a great fast bowler, you need a big heart and a big bottom.

FRED TRUEMAN

THOUGH ESSENTIALLY GOOD-NATURED, HE HAD THAT VITAL WEAPON IN THE FAST BOWLER'S ARMOURY: GRUMPINESS.

Simon Hughes on Angus Fraser

ENGLAND WILL WIN IF CAMILLA PARKER BOWLS.

Australian fans' banner

COACHES
AND
CAPTAINS

Have nothing to do with coaches. In fact, if you should see one coming, go and hide behind the pavilion.

BILL O'REILLY

A man trying to get your legs close together when other men had spent a lifetime trying to get them wider apart.

RACHAEL HEYHOE FLINT ON THE ROLE OF THE PROFESSIONAL CRICKET COACH

PRAY, GOD, NO PROFESSIONAL MAY EVER CAPTAIN ENGLAND.

Martin Hawke

TACTICS

If I had my way, I would take him
to Traitor's Gate and personally
hang, draw and quarter him.

IAN BOTHAM ON RAY ILLINGWORTH

Captaincy is 90 per cent luck and
10 per cent skill. But don't try it
without that 10 per cent.

RICHIE BENAUD

PLAYING AGAINST A TEAM WITH IAN CHAPPELL AS CAPTAIN TURNS A CRICKET MATCH INTO GANG WARFARE.

Mike Brearley

I WAS NEVER COACHED. I WAS NEVER TOLD HOW TO HOLD A BAT.

Donald Bradman

Amateurs have always made, and always will make, the best captains, and this is only natural.

ALLAN GIBSON STEEL

You'll have the most miserable time of your life.

BRIAN CLOSE TO IAN BOTHAM ON CAPTAINCY

COME AGAIN?

The Queen's Park Oval,
exactly as the name suggests,
absolutely round.

TONY COZIER

It's been a very slow and dull day,
but it hasn't been boring. It's been
a good, entertaining day's cricket.

TONY BENNEWORTH

Welcome to Worcester where we have just seen Barry Richards hit one of Basil D'Oliveira's balls clean out of the ground.

BRIAN JOHNSTON

Fred Titmus has two short legs, one of them square.

BRIAN JOHNSTON

ON THE FIRST DAY, LOGIE DECIDED TO CHANCE HIS ARM AND IT CAME OFF.

Trevor Bailey on batter Gus Logie

England have nothing to lose here,
apart from this Test match.

DAVID LLOYD

Yorkshire all out 232, Hutton ill –
I'm sorry, Hutton 111.

JOHN SNAGGE

Turner looks a bit shaky and unsteady, but I think he's going to bat on – one ball left.

BRIAN JOHNSTON

We didn't have any metaphors in my day. We didn't beat about the bush.

FRED TRUEMAN

A VERY SMALL CROWD HERE TODAY. I CAN COUNT THE PEOPLE ON ONE HAND. CAN'T BE MORE THAN 30.

Michael Abrahamson

It is extremely cold here. The England fielders are keeping their hands in pockets between balls.

CHRISTOPHER MARTIN-JENKINS

His throw went absolutely nowhere near where it was going.

RICHIE BENAUD

Matthew Fleming used to be in the Green Jackets, but the way he's batting suggests he'd be better suited in the Light Brigade.

CHARLES COLVILE

Strangely, in slow-motion replay, the ball seemed to hang in the air for even longer.

DAVID ACFIELD

OFF THE
RECORD

If there is a game that attracts the half-baked theorists more than cricket, I have yet to hear of it.

FRED TRUEMAN

They smile and then they stab.

GEOFF BOYCOTT ON CRICKET THEORISTS

Generally, the people out on the pitch are the ones who know how to play the game, not the ones who are writing about it.

MARCUS TRESCOTHICK

I will never be accepted by the snob press.

RAY ILLINGWORTH

Mark Waugh's a great friend of mine and he's got to make a few quid somehow, even by joining you blokes.

SHANE WARNE SPEAKING TO THE PRESS

The media make mountains from molehills to satisfy producers and editors alike.

MARK NICHOLAS

NEWSPAPERS ARE ONLY GOOD ENOUGH FOR WRAPPING UP FISH AND CHIPS.

Martin Crowe

Cricket is full of theorists who can ruin your game in no time.

IAN BOTHAM

You have to try to reply to criticism with your intellect, not your ego.

MIKE BREARLEY ON HANDLING THE MEDIA

THE
BATSMAN
WORE
WHITE

IF YOU CAN'T ALWAYS PLAY LIKE A CRICKETER, YOU CAN AT LEAST LOOK LIKE ONE.

Donald Bradman

White is the colour for the cricket field, so put on your white flannel suit... And your straw hat must be good and shapely, and not fit your head like a beefsteak pudding.

FREDERICK GALE

I look like I do on the field because what I do is knackering.

ANGUS FRASER

THE DAYS OF WOMEN'S CRICKET BEING SEEN AS A KNICKER PARADE MUST BE OVER.

Norma Izard

Capable of looking more dishevelled at the start of a six-hour century than at the end of it.

MARTIN JOHNSON ON MICHAEL ATHERTON

If they want me to get down to twelve stone, I would have to cut off a leg.

IAN BLACKWELL ON THE ENGLAND SELECTORS' ORDERS FOR HIM TO LOSE WEIGHT

IT REQUIRES ONE TO ASSUME SUCH INDECENT POSTURES.

Oscar Wilde on cricket

YOU WILL SOMETIMES SEE A WHOLE FIELDING TEAM RESEMBLING A HERD OF COWS AT PASTURE.

R. C. Robertson–Glasgow on the habit
of cricketers chewing gum

COOL
CRICKETERS

Concentration is sometimes
mistaken for grumpiness.
MICHAEL ATHERTON

Difficult to be more laid-back
without being actually comatose.
FRANCES EDMONDS ON DAVID GOWER

IT'S LIKE WATCHING A SWAN. WHAT YOU SEE ON THE SURFACE BEARS NO RELATION TO THE ACTIVITY GOING ON UNDERNEATH.

David Gower on being accused of being too laid-back

If something is not done to excess,
it's hardly worth doing.

**PETER ROEBUCK COMMENTING ON
IAN BOTHAM'S CHARACTER**

[He's got a] reputation for
being awkward and arrogant,
probably because he is awkward
and arrogant.

FRANCES EDMONDS ON HER HUSBAND PHIL

EEYORE WITHOUT THE *JOIE DE VIVRE.*

Mike Selvey on Angus Fraser

HIS PERSONALITY WAS SUCH THAT IT IS REMEMBERED BY THOSE WHO PLAYED WITH HIM TO THE EXCLUSION OF HIS ACTUAL PERFORMANCE.

John Arlott on W. G. Grace

I regret that my mouth
overtakes my brain.

DERMOT REEVE

He had all the loveable qualities of
a demented rhinoceros.

COLIN McCOOL ON BILL O'REILLY

COMPLETELY STUMPED

Cricket is basically
baseball on Valium.

ROBIN WILLIAMS

Generally regarded as an
incomprehensibly dull and
pointless game.

DOUGLAS ADAMS ON CRICKET

SOMETIMES, PEOPLE THINK IT'S LIKE POLO, PLAYED ON HORSEBACK... ONE GUY THOUGHT IT WAS A GAME INVOLVING INSECTS.

Clayton Lambert

Basically it's just a whole bunch
of blokes standing around
scratching themselves.

KATHY LETTE

★ ★ ★ ★ ★ ★ ★

It's a silly game that nobody wins.

THOMAS FULLER

Personally, I have always looked
on cricket as organised loafing.

WILLIAM TEMPLE

Cricket? It's rubbish.

JUNINHO PAULISTA

There is no more amateurish
professional game in the
world than cricket.

JOHN EMBUREY

I would rather watch a man at his
toilet than on a cricket field.

ROBERT MORLEY

We don't play this game for fun.

WILFRED RHODES

Cricket is the only game where
you can actually put on
weight while playing.

TOMMY DOCHERTY

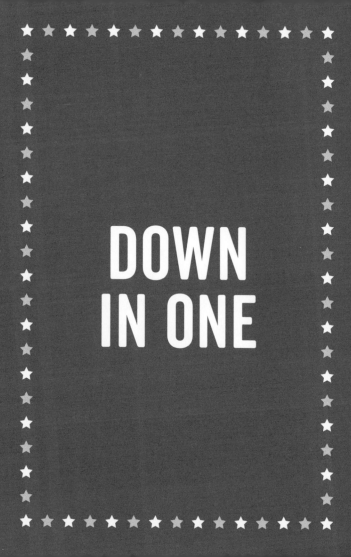

DOWN
IN ONE

It's been 100 days now
so it's quite bizarre.

**DAVID WARNER ON HIS SELF-IMPOSED
ALCOHOL BAN**

To see some of them sink their
drink is to witness performances
as awe-inspiring as ever any
of them displayed on
the cricket field.

IAN BOTHAM

NOTHING YET DEVISED BY MAN IS WORSE FOR A SICK HANGOVER THAN A DAY'S CRICKET IN THE SUMMER SUN.

Michael Parkinson

Let players drink at the beginning
of the game, not after. It always
works in our picnic matches.

PAUL HOGAN ON HOW TO BRIGHTEN UP CRICKET

I find it beautiful to watch and
I like that they break for tea.
That is very cool.

JIM JARMUSCH

I SAID I DON'T DRINK. HE PERSISTED... EVENTUALLY I SAID I WILL HAVE FOUR ICE CUBES. FROM THEN ON IT WAS PRETTY EASY.

Teetotaller Virat Kohli on being asked by Sachin Tendulkar if he'd like a drink

SEX
OVER THE
CENTURIES

Cricket is like sex films. They relieve frustration and tension.

LINDA LOVELACE

I tend to believe that cricket is the greatest thing that God ever created on earth... although sex isn't too bad either.

HAROLD PINTER

I suppose doing a love scene with Raquel Welch roughly corresponds to scoring a century before lunch.

OLIVER REED

I've never got to the bottom of streaking.

JONATHAN AGNEW

IS THERE ANY SEX IN IT?

Peter Sellers, English comedian and actor, as a psychiatrist upon first learning about cricket in *What's New Pussycat?*

IMRAN KHAN HAS BODYGUARDS OUTSIDE HIS ROOM, WARDING WOMEN OFF. I HAVE GUYS WARDING THEM IN.

Zia Mahmood

ATTACKING
SHOTS

Stuff that stiff upper lip crap. Let's
see how stiff it is when it's split.

JEFF THOMPSON

He crossed the line between
eccentricity and idiocy far too
often for someone who was
supposed to be running
English cricket.

IAN BOTHAM ON TED DEXTER

A cricketer – a creature very
nearly as stupid as a dog.

BERNARD LEVIN

David Gower: Do you want
Gatting a foot wider?
Chris Cowdrey: No. He'd burst.

**DURING THE 1985 INDIA V ENGLAND TEST
IN CALCUTTA**

LET'S BE GETTING AT THEM BEFORE THEY GET AT US.

W. G. Grace

BLOODY MEDIEVAL MOST OF THEM.

Ian Botham on the English cricket administration

If someone wore a chocolate bar on his head, Goughie would follow suit.

STEVE OLDHAM ON DARREN GOUGH

Merv Hughes.

STEVE WAUGH ON BEING ASKED TO NAME HIS FAVOURITE ANIMAL

THE MCC SHOULD CHANGE THEIR NAME TO THE MCP.

Diana Edulji calling the MCC male chauvinist pigs after being refused entry to the Lord's Pavilion

THE HOUSE OF 'LORDS'

Do you ask the same question to a male cricketer? Do you ask them who their favourite female cricketer is?

MITHALI RAJ ON BEING ASKED WHO HER FAVOURITE MALE CRICKETER WAS

Say that cricket has nothing to do with politics and you say that cricket has nothing to do with life.

JOHN ARLOTT

A remarkable thing happened at the Sydney Cricket Ground... Many men and youths left the ground expressing astonishment at the remarkably high standard of play and feeling satisfied that they had 'the best bob's worth of cricket for many a day'.

THE *QUEENSLAND MORNING BULLETIN* ON THE ENGLAND V AUSTRALIA 2014 WOMEN'S ASHES MATCH

Cricket can be a bridge and a glue... Cricket for peace is my mission.

MUHAMMAD ZIA-UL-HAQ

CRICKET, LIKE THE UPPER CLASSES AND STANDARDS IN GENERAL, IS IN PERMANENT DECLINE.

Alan Ross

I KNOW WHY HE'S BOUGHT A HOUSE BY THE SEA... SO HE'LL BE ABLE TO GO FOR A WALK ON WATER.

Fred Trueman on Geoff Boycott's move to Poole Harbour

What a magnificent shot!
No, he's out.

TONY GREIG

If it had been a cheese roll, it
would never have got past him.

GRAHAM GOOCH ON MIKE GATTING BEING
BOWLED OUT IN THE 1993 OLD TRAFFORD TEST

I can't bat, can't bowl and can't field these days. I've every chance of being picked for England.

RAY EAST

You should play every game as if it's your last, but make sure you perform well enough to ensure that it's not.

JOHN EMBUREY

Only two problems with our team:
brewer's droop and financial
cramp. Apart from that we ain't
bloody good enough.

CHARLIE PARKER

I can't really say I'm batting badly.
I'm not batting long enough
to be batting badly.

GREG CHAPPELL

THE
WINNER
TAKES
IT ALL

I want to play cricket; it doesn't
seem to matter if you win or lose.

MEAT LOAF

You are only as good as
your last game.

IAN BOTHAM

Cricket is the only game I can enjoy without taking sides.

A. A. MILNE

Any time the West Indies lose, I cry.

LANCE GIBBS

The game you are frightened of
losing is not worth winning.

BENNY GREEN

The aim of English Test cricket is,
in fact, mainly to beat Australia.

JIM LAKER

Some of them are quite nice people, even though they don't win as often as we do.

RACHAEL HEYHOE FLINT ON MALE CRICKETERS

But after all, it's not the winning that matters, is it?

ALASTAIR COOK

I ALWAYS
PLAYED TO WIN.

Hansie Cronje

FROM ASHES TO ASHES

Endless cricket, like endless
anything else, simply
grinds you down.

TED DEXTER

It's not in support of cricket but as
an earnest protest against golf.

**MAX BEERBOHM WHEN ASKED TO CONTRIBUTE
TO W. G. GRACE'S TESTIMONIAL**

I SUPPOSE IT WAS LIKE JOHN MAJOR RUNNING AWAY FROM HIS CIRCUS BACKGROUND TO BE AN ACCOUNTANT.

John Carr on leaving Middlesex
for Barclays bank

Ask me that again when you're all in Dhaka and I'm in Rome, watching Chelsea playing Lazio!

ALEC STEWART ON BEING ASKED IF HE WOULD REGRET RETIRING

I've had about ten operations. I'm a bit like a battered old Escort. You might find one panel left that's an original.

IAN BOTHAM

WICKET
PHILOSOPHY

NINETY PER CENT OF CRICKET IS PLAYED IN THE MIND.

Richard Hadlee

What do they know of cricket who
only cricket know?

C. L. R. JAMES

All is vanity, but cricket.

REV. JOHN MITFORD

WHAT IS HUMAN LIFE BUT A GAME OF CRICKET?

John Sackville

If you're interested in finding out more about our books, find us on Facebook at **Summersdale Publishers** and follow us on Twitter at **@Summersdale**.

www.summersdale.com